UNION PUBLIC LIBRARY

Field Trip!

Bread Bakery

Catherine Anderson

UNION PUBLIC LIBRARY

Heinemann Library
Chicago, Illinois

© 2005 Heinemann Library
a division of Reed Elsevier Inc.
Chicago, Illinois

Customer Service 888-454-2279
Visit our website at www.heinemannlibrary.com

All rights reserved. No part of this publication may be reproduced or transmitted in any form or by any means, electronic or mechanical, including photocopying, recording, taping, or any information storage and retrieval system, without permission in writing from the publisher.

Page layout by Kim Kovalick, Heinemann Library
Printed and bound in China by South China Printing Company Limited.
Photo research by Heather Sabel

09 08 07 06 05
10 9 8 7 6 5 4 3 2 1

Library of Congress Cataloging-in-Publication Data
A copy of the cataloging-in-publication data for this title is on file with the Library of Congress.
  Bread bakery / Catherine Anderson
  ISBN 1-4034-6161-9 (HC), 1-4034-6167-8 (Pbk.)

Acknowledgments
The author and publishers are grateful to the following for permission to reproduce copyright material: p. 4 PhotoDisc/Getty Images; p. 5 Dex Images, Inc./Corbis; pp. 6, 7, 8, 9, 10, 11, 12, 13, 14, 15, 16, 17, 18, 19, 20, 21, 23 Robert Lifson/Heinemann Library

Cover photograph by Robert Lifson/Heinemann Library

Every effort has been made to contact copyright holders of any material reproduced in this book. Any omissions will be rectified in subsequent printings if notice is given to the publisher.

Special thanks to Bruce Turner and employees at Great Harvest Bread Company in Arlington Heights, Illinois.

Special thanks to our advisory panel for their help in the preparation of this series:

Alice Bethke
Library Consultant
Palo Alto, California

Malena Bisanti-Wall
Media Specialist
American Heritage Academy
Canton, Georgia

Ellen Dolmetsch, MLS
Tower Hill School
Wilmington, Delaware

J
641.815
AND
C. 1

Contents

Some words are shown in bold, **like this.**
You can find them in the picture glossary on page 23.

Where Does Bread Come From?

We eat many kinds of bread of all shapes and sizes.

People make bread from **flour**.

You can make bread at home.

Or you can buy bread from
a bakery.

What Do They Use to Make Bread?

Some bakeries make their own **flour**.

They start with **grains** of wheat, called wheat berries.

wheat flour

They grind the wheat berries between two big stones.

The ground wheat berries are wheat flour.

How Is Bread Made?

Bakers mix together **flour,** water, **corn syrup,** and **yeast.**

They mix the ingredients with a big wooden spoon.

yeast

Then, the dough sits in its bowl.

Yeast makes the dough grow bigger.

What Happens Next?

Now the dough has risen a little.

Next, they put more **flour** and salt in the dough.

They mix the dough with a big mixer.

Then, the dough rises again.

When Do They Knead the Dough?

After the dough has risen, it is ready to **knead**.

First, they cut the dough into smaller pieces.

Then, they knead the dough into a shape.

Different kinds of bread come in different shapes.

What Shapes Can Bread Have?

Some bread looks like a big ball.

This baker **kneads** two **loaves**
at once.

Some bread looks like a braid.

This bread looks like a swirl.

Wh n Do Th y Bake the Dough?

After the dough is made into **loaves,** it is baked.

The bread goes into a big, hot oven.

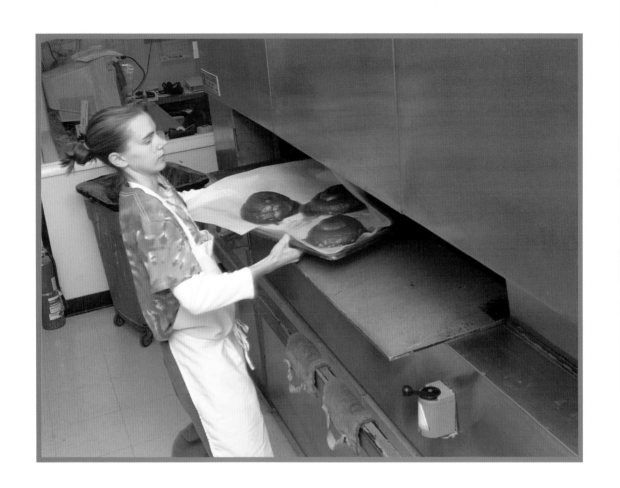

There is a lot of room inside the oven.

How many loaves do you think fit inside?

How Long Does the Bread Bake?

The bread bakes for about half an hour.

When it comes out, it has to cool.

The bread cools on racks.

Then, it is ready to go in bags.

Where Can You Buy the Bread?

You can buy the bread in the bakery shop.

You can taste some of the bread.

You can pick out the bread
you want.

You pay for the bread at the
cash register.

Bakery Map

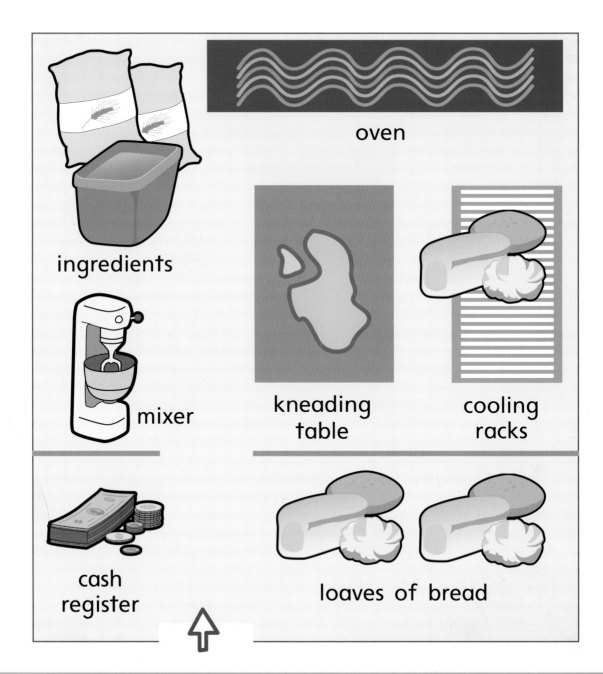

ingredients

oven

mixer

kneading table

cooling racks

cash register

loaves of bread

Picture Glossary

corn syrup
page 8
sugary liquid that is used in cooking

flour
pages 4, 6, 7, 8, 10
ground-up grain used in cooking

grain
page 6
seed of some kinds of grasses, like wheat or oats, that people eat

knead
pages 12, 13, 14
to squeeze and roll dough to give it a shape

loaf
pages 14, 16, 17
shape of bread before it is cut into slices

yeast
pages 8, 9
ingredient in dough that makes it get bigger

Note to Parents and Teachers

Reading for information is an important part of a child's literacy development. Learning begins with a question about something. Help children think of themselves as investigators and researchers by encouraging their questions about the world around them. Each chapter in this book begins with a question. Read the question together. Look at the pictures. Talk about what you think the answer might be. Then read the text to find out if your predictions were correct. Think of other questions you could ask about the topic, and discuss where you might find the answers. Assist children in using the picture glossary and the index to practice new vocabulary and research skills.

Index

FREE PUBLIC LIBRARY UNION, NEW JERSEY

3 9549 00363 1174

UNION PUBLIC LIBRARY